Life Mastery

By
Mark W. Collins

LIFE MASTERY

LIFE MASTERY

Table of Contents

LIFE MASTERY

Chapter 1 – WELCOME

Hello and welcome to Life Mastery, the book!

I, for one, am so excited that you are here!

You have come to the right place at the right time if you are looking for something more, better, greater than what you are currently living.

How can I know that? Simple. I know that because that is the exact reason I first went on my own Life Mastery journey.

I wasn't living a bad life, but I felt "stuck" in not being able to overcome the insecurity that was robbing me of the success, fulfillment, and deep relationships I was desperate for.

I put on a good face and even had success in various things.

I earned my blackbelt because I thought being a "tough guy" would do it.

I received my bachelor's degree because I thought education would do it.

My wife and I started our own business that we sold for a mid-six-figure profit because I thought financial success would do it.

But what nobody else knew was the fear that would wake me up at 3 a.m. or the anxiety that would bubble up inside of me if I made a mistake, said the wrong thing, or made a "bad" decision.

Nobody knew the thoughts I wrestled with that told me I was a failure or that every mistake was a disaster that could bankrupt me and destroy my relationships.

With that background, it should come as no surprise that I have spent countless hours developing, refining, and practicing the Life Mastery strategy, tools, and lifestyle that are detailed in the upcoming pages.

And, just between you and me, I have done that work with you in mind.

You see, I know what it is like to be on the other side of panic. I know what it is like to overcome the debilitating habit of having every mistake be a weapon that you use to beat yourself up. I know what it feels like to be free of the insecurity used to rob you of your self-worth and value.

And I know, with everything in me, that you can experience the same thing.

One of my favorite scriptures is Romans 2:11, which says that "God is no respecter of persons," which means that He loves all of His kids the same.

So, what He has done for me, He can do for you.

With that in mind, why don't we get started? I think that there is no better time than the present to become everything that you were created to be so you can live the life you were created for.

And I am here to coach, mentor, and cheerlead you every step of the way.

Let's get started.

LIFE MASTERY

Chapter 2 – HOW DID WE GET HERE?

Every story has a beginning, and mine started one fall evening in Lincoln, Nebraska. It was there that I was born, the 3rd of 4 children, to my parents, John and Jessie Collins.

We were not wealthy by any means but were a working-class military family.

I was born in Nebraska but was not raised there, which means I missed the chance to grow up as a "corn-fed" country boy in the land of Warren Buffett and Cornhusker football.

My dad was in the United States Air Force, and because of that, we only stayed in Nebraska long enough for my sister to be born exactly one year after I was born.

That's right, my sister was born on my 1st birthday. What a lame gift that was. No knock on my sister. She is a fine person, but how goofy is it that you don't get to have your birthday, not because you have a twin but because your parents have horrible timing.

I am just kidding, of course. Sort of.

While we are sharing, I'll give you another insight into my upbringing.

In my immediate family, I am the only one who does not have a first name that starts with a "J".

That is right, my parents gave each of my sisters a name that starts with a "J". And then I was born, and they called me Mark.

You could assume, because of that, my parents thought one of two things. The first is that I was going to make my own mark.

Sorry, that was too easy.

The other is that my parents looked at me at birth and thought, "Yah, he is going to be the black sheep."

And, if they had thought either of those things, they would have been right.

Of course, all kidding aside, isn't it interesting how choices beyond our control can impact our feelings of worth and Identity? Like being the only "M" in a "J" kind of world, sometimes we can feel like we don't belong, like we are an outsider in our own family, community, or peer group.

One last fun fact from my childhood, since we're sharing.

I already mentioned that my dad was in the military. What I did not mention was, because he was in the military, we had this habit of moving.

To explain to you non-military types, in the military, you are given "assignments" which basically means that your position/job can be needed somewhere else.

And, you guessed it, if your "job" is needed somewhere else, you get to move to that location, state, or country.

For me, that meant that, when I was growing up, I moved with my family to 6 different locations by the time I was 12 years old.

LIFE MASTERY

By the 6th grade, I lived in five states (Nebraska, Oregon, North Dakota, Oklahoma, Utah) and one foreign country (Germany). That is not even including the fact that we lived in 3 different cities in Oklahoma and 2 in Utah.

For those counting, that is an average of a new home, new school, new environment to fit into, and new friends to try to make every other year of my life until the 6th grade.

I am not sure if that led to me being an introverted young man or if I was born that way. What I do know is that moving so much and the lack of long-term relationships had an impact on me.

I don't share that just to let you in on my life but to let you know where I started so you don't have the illusion that I have always been confident and successful. Nothing could be farther from the truth.

But, enough about me.

I have a question for you. The question is, "How did your childhood and your past experiences impact your life, your outlook, and your beliefs?"

You do not have to unpack your whole life here, but I do want you to be aware that you are currently who you are because of one simple thing: the life you have experienced.

I needed to tell you that because, if you are like me, you can sometimes believe the lie that you are "defective" or that you are not as good as others. As if God made either of us with permanent issues or challenges that cannot be overcome.

I also want to tell you clearly right now that I am so sorry for the pain, hurt, and lies you have experienced. They were not your fault and were not right, and I am sorry you had to experience them.

But I also want to tell you that they are not the end of your story.

You need to know that God never demands that you "get over" your pains, hurts, and the lies of your past in order to be acceptable or have the life He intended.

He desires for you not to allow your pains and the lies you have believed to tell you who you are anymore.

As the title of this chapter states, how did we get here?

I know how I "got here" in the brokenness and insecurity from my past that I lived with daily. I also know how I got to the Freedom that is my life now.

And I know that, as you unpack the upcoming chapters, your story can be the same. And the good news is that every lie you bring to the light ceases to have power over you.

I am so excited for your journey into Freedom, healing, and Life Mastery. It is going to be so worth it.

One last thing before we get started for real.

I am so proud of you.

Why? Because it would have been so easy for you to settle for where you are at. But, in just making it this far, I know that you are "betting on yourself," and I am so proud of you for that.

I am inspired by those people who did not have the "overnight success" kind of journey. I love the ones who have been knocked down, had to face considerable obstacles, and made it anyway.

They give me hope when I need it and inspiration to persevere. I wonder if your journey will do that for someone as you work to Master your own Life.

There is a Japanese proverb that states, "Nana korobi, ya oki," which translates to, "Fall down seven times, get up eight." Just vow to keep doing that and you will get to where you are meant to be.

So, now that we are standing, we might as well move forward.

:)

Your future is bright.

Your healing is around the corner.

You have before you everything you need to become the man or woman you were created to be so you can have everything you were created for.

I am all out of "everything's" so let's go.

Chapter 3 - LIFE MASTERY or LIFE MANAGEMENT

Have you ever owned something for an extended period of time and then found out that there was something that you never knew that it could do?

My wife and I bought a van when she owned an in-home daycare. It had all the bells and whistles on it, including a DVD player, power everything, great speakers, etc. It was pretty fancy for the time, and we have "driven the wheels off of that van."

Because it is a reliable vehicle, we have owned it for almost 20 years. To be honest, we have kept it mainly because I am frugal (my wife calls it "cheap") and I love free. And, as you know, once you pay off a vehicle, every year it runs after that is like finding change in your washer, its free money.

So, one day, after owning the van for 15 years, I was in the back, fixing something, when I noticed that, on the sides of the interior walls, there were grocery bag hooks that I had never noticed before.

At that time, we had owned the van for 15 years, and I had a convenient accessory that I had no idea I had access to. Instead, primarily because of the way I drive, we had 15 years of digging cans and produce out from under the bench seat when we got home from grocery shopping because the bags rolled around the back on the way home.

I tell this story to illustrate what has happened in your life and mine.

We have an ability that we have not been aware of, and because of that, we haven't used something that would have made our lives vastly better.

At the risk of being too blunt, we have been fed a lie, and the lie is that we cannot really transform our lives. We can only use habits to manage our lives.

Even in Christianity, we tend to lean towards habits instead of transformation.

This is not to minimize the programs, habits, or traditions that you have been a part of, but I am on a mission to let you know that there is more.

And that "more" is living your life from a place of Life Mastery instead of life management.

It would probably make sense for me to explain what it is that we are aiming for since Life Mastery is the title of this book, as well as the system we are going to be unpacking over the upcoming chapters.

Here is a Truth Bomb for you.

We need an upgrade in our mindset to align with how God has designed us to live instead of living from the lies we have believed. Let me explain.

The "normal" life is typically lived in response to the events that happen. We are brought up, trained even, to respond to the life that happens. It is life by default instead of a life by design.

We come across issues, challenges, or struggles in our lives, and we navigate through the decision-making process to figure out how we are going to deal with them. That is called life management.

But God has not created us to manage the life that happens to us.

In the Word of God, it is clear that we are not created to respond to the life that happens to us but to be the response to the life that is happening around us.

We are not hopeless and helpless creatures who simply have to deal with experiences, but we are the answer to the challenges that present themselves. So why is it that, most of the time, we think we aren't the answer but the question to be figured out?

LIFE MASTERY SCRIPTURE: (Gen. 1:26) "Then God said, "Let Us make man in Our image, according to Our likeness; let them have dominion over the fish of the sea, over the birds of the air, and over the cattle, over all the earth and over every creeping thing that creeps on the earth."."

Not to get too nerdy with you, but the word "Dominion" used in that scripture can also be translated as "Mastery." This means, my friend, that, for you and me, regarding the life that we experience, we are the wave, not the surfer.

As we walk in, so do answers.

As we walk in, so do solutions.

As we walk in, so does the power of God.

Life Mastery is a mindset that believes we are created by God for the life that we are living. It doesn't mean that we do not have challenges. It does mean that who God creates us to be is the answer to whatever circumstance we walk in to.

Even if, for most of our lives, we have lived from a place of life management, from a place of response, it is not too late to change. As a matter of fact, it is always a great time to upgrade your mindset to align with God's word and plan for your life.

YOU WERE CALLED TO LIVE YOUR LIFE BY DESIGN NOT BY DEFAULT.

God created you in His image and likeness, and to repeat it in case you forgot, He did not create you to respond to the life that happens but to be the response to the life that happens.

God's consistent encouragement to us as His children is always to tell us who we are and to remind us about the call on our lives.

I don't want to put your mind on tilt, but you need to realize that God never "fixed" His children so they could manage the issues they were facing. He never said, metaphorically, "Hey, what this van could use are some grocery hooks. We should add them."

What He did do was to reveal who His children were called and created to be so that they lived from the truth instead of from the lies they were told.

For example, Gideon was a mighty man of valor even when he was hiding in a wine press. Moses was the deliverer of Israel, even while he stuttered and asked God to allow his brother to speak for him. Esther was "made for such a time as this," even though she was more worried about her fate than her family and her nation.

Life Mastery, at its core, is simply understanding who we are created to be (Identity) and the life we are created for.

Yes, it all comes back to Identity because Identity is everything.

Who we are created to be versus what our past, pains, and the lies we have believed have told us we were. The basic truth is we are either living as a unique creation or an imitation.

In Genesis 1:26, when God gives us dominion, it is not just over the "birds of the air" and the "fish of the sea". It is also over ourselves.

So, "How do we do that? How do we master ourselves?"

I am glad you asked.

I promise we will be unpacking the answer to that question in the upcoming chapters. But I need to set the table by sharing a foundational truth that we will be working from.

The foundational truth is that anything I teach in Life Mastery starts with the understanding that the Word of God (Bible) is instruction, not philosophy.

Sounds straightforward, doesn't it?

But the truth is, even though it may seem "basic", it isn't always lived out.

What I mean is that, at least in my history with God, more often than not, I tended to read and memorize the Word of God as if it were magical, as if, in just reciting the promises of God, I would magically have them.

The plain truth is that God gave us instructions, not philosophy, and in His word, we can uncover and apply the instructions that result in receiving the promises He has for us.

That is so POWERFUL! I hope you don't read past it without allowing it to sink in.

In wrapping up this conversation, you have a choice to make.

You can live a life of life management and settle for "good enough". We have all had times when we have done that. But now you know that there is a different choice that you can make.

Behind door #2 is the other choice. That choice it to live a life of Life Mastery, even if it takes work. The reward will be the most amazing life you could imagine. A life where you feel like you are living, experiencing, and impacting the world in the exact way you were created to.

A life where you are ready for the challenges, excited for the results, and unwilling to settle for anything less than all you were created for.

A life where you "bet on yourself," and that bet pays off with a life beyond what you could have imagined. A life of Life Mastery.

LIFE MASTERY

Chapter 4 - IDENTITY REVEALED

Growing up in a military family, my upbringing could be considered disciplined. In fact, I tell people, in describing my father, that he wasn't a drill instructor, but he would have made a good one. He did the best he knew how, having grown up without a father, but he was, for me, someone who I feared.

Growing up, I remember my dad telling my sisters and me the stories about his "single days" and the drunken fights he got into. He was a tough man, in no small part, because he raised himself and his younger brother when his mother moved him and his brother to Oregon to get away from her abusive husband.

Hearing his stories painted a clear picture for me as to what it was to be a man. The challenge for me was that being an introverted and, to be honest, insecure young man, I knew that I did not measure up. The idea of a fight scared the "you know what" out of me, and being the "new kid" everywhere we moved didn't help in trying to be that guy who commanded attention like my dad did.

With that picture of manhood, you know, the "real men don't cry" kind of picture, I tried to find a way to fill in what was missing. I had no idea what was missing, I just knew something was. And so, I began my quest to become more than who I saw when I looked in the mirror.

I took courses, read books, and studied martial arts. I tried relationships. I worked on confidence. I worked on belief. I worked on physical abilities. However, I came to find out that there is a difference between adopting habits and creating transformation.

I had no idea what transformation was or that I needed it. What I did know was that what I was doing to change my life, the habits I was adopting, and the affirmations I was reciting did not work. I would study and implement the habits of successful people, but there was something inside of me that told me, "You aren't like that guy".

Don't get me wrong, I accomplished some quality goals, including a 2nd-degree black belt, a Bachelor's degree, business ownership, etc. The problem was that what I did on the outside didn't overcome the feelings and voices on the inside telling me I didn't measure up and that I wasn't as good as everyone else.

I found that, in looking for a change, I would adopt a new habit to change an old one. And, as long as I kept up the new habit, I could sustain the change I was looking for.

But don't you know that the minute you stop that habit, what happens to the change you desire?

It goes away.

The interesting thing is, come to find out, God never invited us to change but instructed us to transform.

LIFE MASTERY SCRIPTURE: (Romans 12:2)
"And do not be conformed to this world, but be transformed by the renewing of your

mind, that you may prove what is that good and acceptable and perfect will of God."

You see, you are not meant to acquire different habits to change a behavior.

You are instructed by God to be transformed by renewing your mind. Really to align your mind/thoughts to be like God's.

And, if you do that, you won't need to manage your life with habits. You will simply live from that place of transformation.

It is actually pretty simple.

It comes down to this. God isn't telling you that you need to change to become somebody different. He is telling you that you need to transform to become who you were created to be, to begin with.

For me, the truth was that I was never meant to be my dad. There was already one of those in the world.

I know you may be having some doubts, so let me go a little deeper, if that is okay.

The word "transformed" in Romans 12:2 is the Greek word "metamorphoo" from which we get the word metamorphosis. We use that word to describe the change a caterpillar makes into a butterfly.

The interesting thing about that change is that their appearance changes, but, if you were to take a strand of DNA from a caterpillar and a strand of DNA from it as a butterfly and look at them under a microscope, you would see that they are exactly the same.

I found out in my own Life Mastery journey that God is not changing us so that we are better but revealing us so that we see that we are already enough.

The truth is that who God created you to be makes all the difference in the world.

It all comes down to IDENTITY.

Anyone who has been around me long enough will hear me say, "Identity is Everything."

The life change you and I are looking for. The person that you desire to be. The things that you desire to accomplish. They are all determined by who you believe you are.

Who you believe you are is the person who will show up at your business, your marriage, your relationships, at your church, in your family, activities, and life.

So, the first thing to do to make a change in your life is to get clarity on this one thing: who did God create you to be?

Identity can be defined in a few ways.

Identity is Innate

You were born with your Identity intact. The challenge is that your experiences, pains, hurts, and disappointments have told you that you were someone else. Someone less.

Less successful. Less valuable. Less worthy. Less loved.

But what if your life has lied to you, and you actually are more than that?

LIFE MASTERY

Identity is Created

In forming you in your mother's womb, God created you with a unique Identity that is specific and perfectly you. He formed you with intention. He formed you with vision. He formed you with planning and purpose and perfectly for the life you were created to live.

Identity is the Key to Happiness, Hope & Fulfillment

Unless you know who, you are, you will show up as who you believe you are supposed to be.

And nobody wins when that happens.

It is not "fake it till you make it." It is "find it so you can fulfill it."

Fulfillment comes from the life we are living aligning with who we are created to be. It is a feeling of having a life that matters, a life that has an impact.

What it comes down to is the truth that you can either live your life from the person you were created to be (Identity) and have that person affect your experiences for your benefit.

Or you can live your life from the experiences of your past, allowing them to determine who you believe you are (Identity) and the life you are capable of.

And, just to let you in on a little secret, that second choice is how I was living my life and how the majority of us live our lives.

We allow our hurts, pains, disappointments, and the lies we have believed to tell us who we are.

Because of that, we shrink back from the adventure that God has in store for us. The life of abundance and fulfillment.

The life we were created for.

What if you didn't tolerate that "less than" life any longer?

What if you said "yes" to God and "no" to the lies?

What if you said "yes" to the life you are created for and "no" to the fear holding you back?

What if you said "yes" to an absolutely, unmistakably fulfilling life and "no" to just getting by?

What if you said "yes" to the truth of who you are and "no" to the lie that you are not worth it, not valued, not as good as everyone else, not meant for happiness, not meant for joy, peace, fulfillment, and life?

You can do it. It is one decision away.

It all starts with the answer to the question, "Who are you?" The answer to that one question will change your life forever

If you haven't heard it yet, I need to tell you that you are more than the life you have lived so far. I know that you may have accomplished some things that you should rightfully feel proud of. But I am here to tell you that there is more.

It is my belief that the question of who we are actually starts with this internal wrestling match that happens when we believe that there is more for us then what we are living.

There is this voice that we can't shake that says, "Isn't there more than this?"

That is the real you crying out. It is the Spirit on the inside saying, "I am more than these limitations and lies I am believing. I am more than my finances, my job, my failures, my level of success."

And the good news is that you are right. There is more for you then what you've seen so far. There is more to your life then what you have experienced.

It may be hidden because of the anxiety, fears, insecurity, or imposter syndrome you are battling if you are anything like I was. But, and this is a huge but, you have been created for more than those things standing in your way.

And there is no better time than the present to reveal it.

LIFE MASTERY

LIFE MASTERY SCRIPTURE: (Psalm 139:14
- 15) "I will praise You, for I am
fearfully and wonderfully made; Marvelous
are Your works,
And that my soul knows very well.
(15) My frame was not hidden from You,
When I was made in secret, And skillfully
wrought in the lowest parts of the earth.

There is a great picture of what the Life Mastery journey looks like in the life of Michelangelo.

If you are not aware, Michelangelo was an artist who lived in the late 1400s and early 1500s.

He was known for creating many paintings and frescos (paintings on walls and ceilings), but his favorite medium to use was sculpture.

He made several beautiful marble sculptures, and one of his most famous was the sculpture of David. It was stated, at the time of its completion, that it was the most perfectly sculpted human form ever sculpted.

Michelangelo was asked one time about how he sculpted one of his sculptures, and his response was, "I saw the angel in the marble and carved until I set him free."

That, in a nutshell, is the Life Mastery journey.

It is chipping away at the marble of lies, fears, insecurities, and doubts until what is revealed is the person you were created to be.

God has created you uniquely, specifically, and perfectly, and the more you discover who you are created to be, the more you will live the life you were created for.

And the more you will see how amazing God is in specifically, personally, and passionately investing in your creation.

You are not an accident, arbitrary, or a copy.

There is an innate, God-given Identity that is the true you.

LIFE MASTERY

Whether you understand it, believe it, or live from it, it is still on the inside to be discovered.

You are better than you think you are.

You are more than you have experienced.

You are greater than you could imagine.

Let's invest in seeing that person come to life.

LIFE MASTERY

Chapter 5 – YOUR CHARACTER IS YOUR CALLING

As a teenager, I started taking martial arts. The motivation for doing that was partly from seeing movies where this undefeatable "good guy" put a beat down on all of the "bad guys" who totally deserved it.

And, to be honest, part of the motivation was to try and live up to who my dad showed that a man should be. I thought my dad was fearless, and his stories of fighting when he was a young adult painted an image for me of what a man should be.

The problem was, that wasn't me. I was afraid of confrontation, and getting into a fight was the last thing I wanted to do. So, in my eyes, if I could become a black belt, then I would be fearless and would be able to intimidate instead of being intimidated. And I would meet the definition I had of what a man should be.

As you already know, that didn't work. And it didn't work for the very reason we will talk about in this chapter.

In the last chapter, we just finished unpacking Identity. And, in doing it, believe it or not, we unearthed a challenge.

Do you want to know what it is?

The challenge with telling people to invest time into discovering their Identity is that most of the time, our definition can be a little bit off.

What do I mean?

Let me give you an example.

If I were to ask you to describe yourself, and you were like most people, the first things you would list off would be things you do or have done, the career you have, and accomplishments you have completed.

"I am a doctor." "I went to Columbia Med school." "I like hiking and chasing butterflies." "I am a Pulitzer Prize winner in anthropology." "I am a husband and father".

The issue with these responses is that they are all responses of what you have accomplished, not who you are.

Maybe not those phrases exactly, but we all have our list.

You see, when we talk about Identity, most people, most of the time, list what they do, not who they are.

There is a difference.

Who you are created to be, the amazing "you" on the inside, is not summed up in your activities and accomplishments. Your activities and accomplishments are just aspects of your Identity lived out.

I know, I know, you are saying, "Mark, I know that I am more than my job, accomplishments, or net worth."

We know it intellectually, but then that leads to the question, "If we know it, why aren't we living it?"

I'll tell you why I wasn't living it.

The reason I wasn't living it was that I didn't believe it. I could say I did and even nod my head when someone recited the truth to me. The issue was that I didn't know my Identity, and, in the absence of that understanding, I was left to grab whatever I could to prove that I was a person of value and worth.

But none of the things I "grabbed" were ever enough to overcome the insecurity and imposter syndrome telling me that I wasn't good enough.

It is interesting that the things that are easy to rely on for your Identity are typically your career, accomplishments, and net worth. The same things the world identifies with value.

So, when you use them to inform Identity, what happens if you lose your job, or you miss the target on a goal, or there is a down turn in the economy that impacts your net worth?

If your Identity is tied to your activities, then you are handcuffed to the results.
And, when the results are less than perfect, they negatively impact your sense of worth and value.

Then, your thoughts and emotions take a dive and lead to imposter syndrome, anxiety, or insecurity.

You need to understand that your Identity is more than your activities, so if things aren't "up to par" in an area of your life, it doesn't reflect on your value. It is simply an experience you are walking through.

I am here to make you aware of that because if, like me, you are a Christian, the Bible is very clear that you have a calling on your life. The challenge is when you think your calling is a title, job, or income level, then you are limited by the result of that.

LIFE MASTERY

The truth that most people do not realize is that your Character is your calling.

You are not a mess that needs to be fixed. You are a Masterpiece that needs to be revealed.

LIFE MASTERY SCRIPTURE: (Romans 12:2) "And do not be conformed to this world, but be transformed by the renewing of your mind, that you may prove what is that good and acceptable and perfect will of God."

When God invites us into our transformational journey, it is not so we can know His will for the world alone but so we can know His will for us.

And a huge part of that is "changing your mind" about who you are created to be.

When you do that, you will be able to clearly see who you have been created to be so you can have the life you are created for.

Sometimes we are asking God to do for us what He has already done in us.

If I am a new creation, then what does that person look like, act like, talk like? That person lived out is your character.

Just to be clear, that doesn't mean that you need to change to become a different person. It means that you are invited to have a different focus.

You see, God is not in the business of changing His children. If they needed to be changed, that would mean that God was not perfect in creating them, and that is a lie.

You need to let that sink in.

So, because of that understanding of God and our focus, we can look at Life Mastery, and the transformation Romans 12:2 invites us to.

And the best way to start that understanding of who we are is by reminding ourselves who God is. If God is perfect, then that means all He creates is perfect. I understand about our being "born into iniquity (sin)," as the Bible says, but stay with me for a moment.

If God is perfect and His creation is as well, then if I demean myself, think less of myself, put myself down, then I am demeaning, thinking less of and putting down the God who created me.

So, while God didn't change His children, He did change their names to align with who they were created to be and the impact they were created to have.

Whether it was Peter, Isaac, Abraham, Paul, etc., God gave each a name that matched their calling, destiny, and the life they were created to live. He did not give them a name and then change them to live up to that name.

God is in the business of bringing clarity when you are living less than who He created you to be.

At the end of the day, your Character leads to your calling. Your calling does not lead to your character.

Sometimes, we are striving to prove who we are instead of investing because of who we are.

By understanding that, you will stop living for your job, title & income. You will be able to align with who you are created to be, not live from who you are not.

That is what Freedom looks like.

And that transformation happens through a relationship with God, not through the right habits.

There is a difference between having habits to become someone versus having habits because you are someone.

In a relationship with God, you discover who you are created to be, and your habits naturally come from your character.
To be honest, apart from a relationship with God, your habits are a cheap substitute for the relationship.

LIFE MASTERY

Sometimes, we can have the issue of believing that we have to measure up to be worthy, but until we discover that we are worthy, we will never measure up.

God is trying to cast our vision higher, to elevate our understanding of the purpose behind the journey.

LIFE MASTERY SCRIPTURE: (Gen. 1:26) "Then God said, 'Let Us make man in Our image, according to Our likeness; let them have dominion over the fish of the sea, over the birds of the air, and over the cattle, over all the earth and over every creeping thing that creeps on the earth'."

You are the prize. If you start there, you will see that you are not just good enough but everything you need to be for the life He has created for you and created you for.

And, if you start there, everything, absolutely everything in your life will change forever.

LIFE MASTERY

Chapter 6 – EXPAND YOUR CAPACITY

There is a demonstration I saw one time where a teacher took a large jar and filled it full of medium-sized, grey river rocks.

He then asked his students if the jar was full, and the students said with certainty that it was.

Then, the teacher took a plastic bag filled with sand and poured it into the jar, watching as the sand filtered down through the rocks, filling in the spaces between them.

He then asked the students again if the jar was full, and again, the students said with certainty that it was.

Then, the teacher took a pitcher of lukewarm water and poured it into the jar. The water filled the jar, submerging the rocks and sand that were previously placed in the jar.

The teacher then, for the last time, asked the students if the jar was full, and the students answered with certainty that it was.

My question is this: when were the students right?

The answer depends on your belief about the capacity of the jar.

With that picture in mind, my question for you is, what do you have on the inside of you?

What life are you created to live?

What activities are you equipped to accomplish?

What impact are you meant to make?

There is this thing that many of us do, myself included.

We can sometimes unintentionally leave some "gas in the tank." Or should I say, "room in the jar".

LIFE MASTERY

We don't reach super high or try with all we've got because we don't always know if we can accomplish the "big things" in life.

And, without that assurance, it can feel safer to give a half effort and believe that you could have succeeded rather than give everything, fall short, and have to deal with the thoughts of failure that creep into your mind.

But what if God designed you for more?

What if He wants you to live at the highest level that you were created for, not the level you are comfortable with?

LIFE MASTERY SCRIPTURE: (Mark 10:10)
"I have come that they may have life, and that they may have it more abundantly."

Life more abundantly is not a life of safety and comfort. It is a life of radical alignment with who God created you to be and the life He created you for.

Just to be clear, the more abundant life is not

me telling you that you are guaranteed to be a millionaire.

It also does not mean that all of life will be roses and butterflies.

A life of abundance is really a life of fulfillment, and that life is not without challenges. It is, however, a life that perfectly aligns with who you are created to be and the life you are created for.

And, to be completely honest, it is the only life that will give you fulfillment.

So, what does that life look like lived out?

What is the "perfect level" of life that God has for you?

It is not just about your Identity and your Character but your Capacity.
The opposite of Capacity is living less then what you are capable of. And you know you are there when you have this gnawing voice inside screaming, "There has got to be more!"

LIFE MASTERY

In discovering our Identity and unpacking our Character, there is the continual unfolding idea that if God has created us perfectly, then what does that life look like lived out?

It is the restoration of our dreams.

It is the rekindling of that inner fire.

It is betting on the possibility that we can have it all.

It is believing again.

Not because you are arrogant or full of yourself but because you believe God when He says that He has thoughts (plans) He thinks towards you, to give you a future and a hope.

LIFE MASTERY SCRIPTURE: (Jer. 29:11) "For I know the thoughts that I think toward you, says the Lord, thoughts of peace and not of evil, to give you a future and a hope."

In order to correctly discern what life God has created us to live, we need to engage Him, believe Him, and adopt a mindset aligned with Him.

Anything less than that can look more like arrogance than humility.

As we said in a previous chapter, in believing less about ourselves and our lives, we believe less of God and the truth He speaks.

The opposite of that is what it looks like to live from a "renewed mind".

It means to think thoughts that align with what He says, not what we have experienced or what we have been told about ourselves.

Imagine if the truth of His word were louder than the lies you believed. What would change in your life? What would change in your thinking? What would change in your activities?

With all of this in mind, I have another

question for you.

What is the level of Capacity God has created you to live out?

And, not to question you to death, my follow-up question for you would be, "What can you do to stretch your Capacity to be able to steward more and more of it in your life?"

It comes down to this: we are only going to live at the highest level we are created for if we actively reach beyond what is comfortable.

It is like working out. Your abilities grow through resistance. To grow your muscles, you have to introduce them to something that is not comfortable, and it may even be hard. But, in doing the exercise, the muscle grows. As does your Capacity.

If you put time into your relationships and your role within them, then those relationships get deeper.

If you put time into educating yourself on

financial management, you will gain the tools and ability to manage and increase your income.

Capacity comes down to 3 things.

The first thing is a belief in and an openness to living out the fullness of the Capacity you were created for.

That means taking the "shackles" off. It means getting beyond the walls of insecurity that you use to protect yourself. It means having a willingness to heal what is standing in the way of your Freedom.

The second thing is getting a clear vision of life at the level God created you for.

Many times, our biggest issue is that we think we are "one of many" rather than "one of a kind." We want to fit in, and we look to those around us to see what success is supposed to be.
But you are not the sum total of the people you are around unless you let yourself be.

The third thing is to put time into the tools, teaching, and habits that increase your Capacity.

There is a reason why we don't dig a trench with a screwdriver. It is the wrong tool for the job.

The right tool is all about implementation and impact.

And come to find out, two things determine implementation with impact.

They are investing time and effective tools. If you put a consistent time investment into using effective tools, you will get the results you dream about.

What is your Spiritual Capacity? What is the level of relationship with God that you were created for? Is there more then what you have currently experienced?

What is your Relational Capacity? What is the level of intimacy, connectedness, vulnerability, and authenticity that you were created for?

What is your Vocational Capacity? What is the impact you were created to have in the world through your job, business, invention, or activity?

What is your Physical Capacity? What is the level of physical and intellectual fitness that you were created to have for your life?

What is your Financial Capacity? What are the areas of investment that God has created you for that honor Him and bless you?

The clearer your vision of who you are created to be and the life you are created for, the more your Capacity becomes clear.

And the more your vision becomes clear, the more you will find the resources to increase Capacity towards your created level.

Which leads to seeing your Capacity grow. Keep your eyes focused forward and focused up. There is a God-level life in store for you, and it is one belief away.

Chapter 7 - I WILL UNTIL

When my youngest daughter was born, my wife and I felt that it was important to have 100% of her care done by us. This meant that, even though both of us worked, we were going to find a way to make it happen.

The first phase of our plan was for me to change shifts at work to the night shift, allowing me to take care of our baby during the day while my wife was at work.

As a quick sidebar, the second phase was to purchase a home and open an in-home daycare, which we did, resulting in some challenges but also great success.

Anyways, back to the story at hand. Because I worked at night, when I got home, I would wind down by watching TV and, come to find out, the TV after midnight had a lot of the get-rich-quick and miracle cure programs.

In watching them at night, I would find

myself ready to be all in on a bunch of things, whether it was buying real estate with no money down, losing weight without changing my diet or exercising, investing part-time to make millions, or becoming fluent in a language in two months or less.

The theme of all of the "infomercials" was pretty much the same.

There was a sales tactic that drew you into signing contracts, paying significant amounts of money, and investing large chunks of time.

It is the "secret formula" or "magic pill" sales tactic telling you that you could get "A" (the physique, money, or Freedom) without having to put in a bunch of work or time. You simply need to acquire "B" (their secret formula or "quick fix" program) that they are selling.

Those strategies, in most cases, turn out to be more hype than truth. But I am here to tell you that there is a secret that, if you implement it, will give you the results you are looking for.

I say "secret" not because I have uncovered something that no one else knows but because most people don't realize that it is something that is necessary.

And the truth is, it has nothing to do with something that you have to purchase, invest in, or sign up for. It is all about something inside of you and how you can align with a powerful tool for your own success.

Coincidentally, it is a common trait I recognized in every person of great success that I read about or studied.

This "secret" I am referring to is a mindset that will make the difference between achieving great success or not.

In the context of our conversation in these chapters, it is the difference between Mastering your life and managing it.

To dispel some myths, the key to success is not having an easier path, more money, the perfect strategy, or the best upbringing.

LIFE MASTERY

The single mindset that can lead you to the success that you desire is simply the unwillingness to give up until your goal is achieved.

You can call it tenacity, focus, "stick-to-it-iveness," or any number of other things, but when you peel away the layers, at the core is a belief that you are meant for the outcome you are striving for and a refusal to give up until you get it.

To put a name on it, it is an "I will until" mindset.

I know, I know. It sounds simple, and you are saying, "Of course, I will do that."

But I would not be a good coach/mentor if I didn't tell you the truth that everyone says they won't give up until they run into the first challenge.

Like Mike Tyson famously said, "Everyone has a plan until they get punched in the mouth."

And, if you are striving for a Life Mastery life, you will get punched in the mouth.

Successful people, Life Masters, aren't successful because their goals are easy. They never are.

They are successful because they have determined that their goal is worth overcoming the things that aren't easy.

IF YOUR GOAL IS EASY THAN YOUR GOAL IS TOO SMALL FOR YOU.

To let you in on a truth bomb, it is not really about the goal itself but betting on yourself as you strive to achieve it.

It is a belief that you are worth fighting for. It is an understanding that the person you are created to be is worth investing in. It is an unwillingness to compromise on that belief until you see it come to pass.

It doesn't mean that success happens without adjustments or modifications to your strategy. "I will until" isn't blindly doing the same thing over and over again that is not working. It is refusing to give up on your goal and yourself even if, at first, you don't succeed.

LIFE MASTERY

I have never succeeded the very first time I have attempted something big, and, to be honest, I do not know anyone who has.

The truth is that the "overnight" success is a myth. The only people who are overnight successes are those who finally have the spotlight on them when their success has been achieved. No one paid attention or focused on them while they spent countless hours honing their craft or developing their skill or product.

For every actor who has a successful role, there are hundreds and thousands of hours they have spent practicing their craft and being coached with no audience or applause.

For every person who has invented something revolutionary, there are thousands of times the invention failed to work.

But, with all of the challenges and "roadblocks" there is this something, this "nagging" on the inside that cannot be denied, and it lets you know that there is more for you than where you are currently at.

Life Mastery can get you from where you are to Freedom, but it is not a magic formula, just a proven one. It only works if you work it. And the only way you will work it, no matter the "highs" or "lows," is by determining that you will not give up.

"But Mark," you say, "How do I do that?"

Great question!

Here are a couple of steps I recommend for you to implement to have an "I will until" mindset.

The first is to keep the prize in mind. By continuously reminding yourself of the goal you have, you create focus on what matters.

As I tell people, it is really the "why" behind the "what."

What is that undeniable fire on the inside of you?

What is that passion that cannot be satisfied with anything else?

What is that belief that will not go away?

What did you enter this journey for? It wasn't because you had some extra time or were looking for something to do.

What is it that you want to overcome? What is it that you want to live out? Who is the man or woman that you believe you were created to be, even if you have not seen it yet?

Is it to be that person in your relationships or job?

Is it to be that person in your business or family?

Is it to honestly, authentically connect with your God?

Is it to have the level of income that you are created to steward?

What is your "I will until" goal?

LIFE MASTERY

LIFE MASTERY SCRIPTURE:

(Eph.2:10) "For we are His workmanship, created in Christ Jesus for good works, which God prepared beforehand that we should walk in them..."

Having an "I will until" mindset is about being tenacious on your behalf.

It is about being unwilling to give up on yourself.

It is about saying, "I am going to live from the truth of who I am created to be, not the insecurity (or fear or worry or anxiety; or anger, or control) that I have had."

Even when the results do not match the effort.

There are times in your Life Mastery journey when your results are the opposite of what you hoped for.

Be willing to move forward even then.

LIFE MASTERY

The second thing I recommend is for you to be vulnerable enough to allow yourself to be coached/mentored through the journey.

While there is value in walking out your own journey, there is also power in having people in your life who are on the same journey and can encourage you with their hard-earned, battle-tested wisdom.

There is a saying that says, "Knowledge is learning from your mistakes. Wisdom is learning from the mistakes of others."

It is not only wisdom you gain but an acceleration toward success when you surround yourself with people who have been where you are and who can show you how to get where they are at.

It is powerful.

It is encouraging.

It is wisdom.

There is a story I have heard in various forms that applies to our conversation. It is the story of a group of Spaniards who landed in Central America.

The leader knew that they had an incredibly hard journey ahead, so when all the men came ashore, he gave the order to have their boats burned. When asked by his men why he did it, he said that now they would have no other option but to move forward.

This is a "burn the boats" time for you.

Burning the boats of compromise.

Burning the boats of giving up.

Burning the boats of giving in to comfort, to ease, to whatever.

Give yourself no alternative to Freedom, and you will have the Freedom you want.

The goal of Life Mastery is to be who you were created to be so you can have the life that you were created for. It is a declaration that every one of us announces that says "I am going to be who God says I am no matter what."

LIFE MASTERY

I am here to mentor, coach, teach, be a friend, and cheerlead you.

But no one will give a greater investment than you do.

Determine you are worth it, and let's do this.

Chapter 8 – MASTERING YOUR THOUGHTS

Have you ever wondered what the secret was to actually be transforming your life? Sure, there are good habits you can incorporate and checklists you can make to get things done, but transformation is a different thing altogether.

I know because I have done the "habit and checklist thing," and they just left me a slave to my habits and checklists instead of a slave to my struggle. Neither one brought Freedom.

If I am reading you right, it is a desire you have to be transformed instead of managed. And, maybe, like I was, you just have no clue where to begin.

Maybe you tried the standard things like memorizing some scriptures or adopting a new and "healthy" habit. But, after doing it for some time, you feel like you're right back where you started.

LIFE MASTERY

I remember being in my twenties and knowing with everything I had inside of me that, I was created for more than the life I was living and the decisions I was making.

I invested in personal development, expecting a miracle but receiving marginal improvement.

There came a time, for me, when enough finally became enough.

I had tried everything that I knew and applied all the things that I read and studied, and I still struggled with self-doubt and fear.

I wasn't rich yet.

I wasn't confident yet.

I wasn't irresistibly attractive yet.

I wasn't successful yet.

I am kidding just a little about the "irresistibly attractive" part, but the truth was that I didn't have the promises that were given, and I had run out of ideas on how to get different results.

I was a Christian by that time, which, if I can be honest, only added another layer of pressure because there were promises in God's word that added to the list of things I did not have.

But, through all of the tears of frustration and "baby step" results, I started to move forward. I started to be set free one truth at a time.

Through that journey, I started to piece together some phenomenal revelation and strategy that became the Life Mastery program that this book is based on.

There was one pivotal discovery that fueled my own Life Mastery journey. I may have heard it before, but this time, it took hold of me.

What I discovered was that there is a starting point for all transformation. It is not complicated, but, for most of us, we are unaware that it is there.

The drum roll moment was this: all transformation starts with…

Mastering your Thoughts.

Seems pretty straightforward, but it is not simple.

There is no word we have spoken, or action we have taken that has not first started with a thought. In fact, there is nothing that has been created, developed, or launched that was not first a thought in someone's head.

The start of transformation, really the foundation of it, is in Mastering your Thoughts, period.

I know that that is a bit of a mind shift to most of us because, if you are like me, you had no idea that you had a choice to do anything but manage the voices, the noises, and the negativity that is sometimes in our heads.

We typically live a life of fighting against those "random" thoughts that come in with inappropriate ideas at inopportune times.

We have a hard time just managing our thoughts, let alone mastering them.

Do you relate?

It is that internal dialogue that tells you, "I'm going to fail" or "He/she doesn't love me." We all have an inner dialogue that sometimes tells us who we are not and what we won't have. It can be that voice of doubt when you are going for an interview or asking someone out. It can be the internal dialogue beating you up for something you did or didn't do.

If it is something you have ever struggled with, I have a question for you, "What if you don't have to struggle with it? What would that mean to you?"

LIFE MASTERY SCRIPTURE: (Proverbs 23:7) "As he thinks in his heart, so is he."

(PS. 19:14) "Let the words of my mouth and the meditation of my heart be acceptable in Your sight, O Lord, my strength and my Redeemer."

There are three things I need you to be aware of as we are unpacking Mastering your Thoughts.

The first is that when you think of "thoughts" in biblical terms, you should think of "meditation." When God is speaking of meditation, it is your thoughts or thought life that He is referring to.

So, when He is speaking of the "meditations of my heart," it is the inner dialogue that He wants to instruct you about.

The second is that the example of Proverbs 23:7 references a "rich man" whose actions are deceiving. He is acting one way, but inside, he is a different person.

That is exciting to know because the instruction that God is giving us in those verses is that if we want to become the person we are created to be, it first starts with our thoughts.

That should "**explode**" in your heart because what that means is that you are in the driver's seat of your own transformation.

You can literally transform your mind by putting focused effort into Mastering your Thoughts.

Is anyone else losing their mind with this!?!

Come on, my friend!

When I figured that out, I knew that I had found **the key** to unlocking everything I believed for in my life.

As I said at the beginning of our conversation, for years, I had a GIGANTIC desire to be the person I believed I was, not the person I showed up as. And I had tried a bunch of things, but none gave me the resulting "Freedom" God promised.

But, when the truth of transformation was "dropped on me", I knew that I was going to be able to do this.

The third thing I want to make you aware of is the full transformational strategy.

The foundation and first step is Mastering your Thoughts. There are, however, two other components to transformation. Those components are Mastering your Words and Mastering your Actions.

All of the transformations that people create in their lives are done through Mastering their Thoughts, Words, and Actions.

What I tell my students is, *"What you think, you will say. What you say, you will do. What you do, you will become."*

It is as simple and as hard as that.

Just so you know, we will unpack mastering your words and actions in the next couple of chapters, but I wanted to introduce those components now rather than have you feel that I am giving you the "Wait, but there's more" kind of vibe as we introduce them in the upcoming pages.

In unpacking the subject of Mastering your Thoughts, you need to understand this secret.

The secret is that you are already using your thoughts to shape your life. You just haven't known that you are doing it.

The truth bomb I am dropping in your lap is that we are where we are in our lives because of the thought life we have had.

You see, the strategy of changing your life by changing your thoughts isn't really new because you have been creating your life with your thoughts.

It's not exciting to hear sometimes, but it is good to know.

Just to be clear, your thoughts lead the way in shaping your life, and they also lead the way in transforming your life.

The difference between the two is the difference in living your life by design or by default.

Remember the second chapter where we talked about life management or Life Mastery? We talked about living life by design, not by default.

It can be thought of like this: you are either the driver or the passenger in the car of your thoughts.

In the context of "thoughts," that looks like either managing your thoughts by fighting off the "bad ones" as they come up or Mastering your Thoughts by choosing the thoughts that you will allow and ones that focus on the truth of who you are and the life you are created for.

And the quickest way to know if you are Mastering or managing is to ask yourself, "What am I thinking?"

When times are stressful. When you are bored. When things aren't going right. When you get in a fight with your spouse. When you make a mistake. When you are searching for direction.

What are your thoughts?

Because your thoughts will always align with who you believe you are.

That is why we started our journey in this book, with Identity.

If you do not know who you are, your experiences will tell you.

Let me demystify this a little by explaining how our thoughts create the life we live.

The first way our thoughts create our lives is by shaping (and reshaping) our understanding of the experiences of our lives. Our thoughts interpret the ups and downs, victories and failures, challenges and successes of our life.

You fail a test, you end a relationship, you win an award, or you get a promotion. Your interpretation of every experience is a function of your thoughts.

Because of that, your past experiences and the way you interpret them (think about them) inform your present experiences. Basically, your past is the filter through which you judge your present experience.

It is actually a part of God's perfect creation. He has created your brain to protect and prosper you, and that is done through interpreting your environment and the experiences you have.

In the ancient past, interpretation gave our ancestors the ability to avoid animals that would eat them and plants that would poison them. Nowadays, we use it mostly to avoid things that will make us uncomfortable.

The second way our thoughts create our lives is by clarifying who we are created to be.

Your thoughts not only interpret your experiences but, more importantly, define who you believe you are.

The issue isn't necessarily whether your experiences are good or bad, happy or painful. We all have them.

The issue is that our thoughts will always answer the question, "What does this experience say about me?"

I am not diminishing the impact that negative experiences have had on your life, but the truth is, the pain hasn't made you who you are today. The interpretation of the painful experience has made you who you are today.

I say pain, but it could also have been a success or accomplishment as well as a trauma or disappointment. The truth is that every experience engages your thoughts for an interpretation, and each of them helps create an Identity for you.

The problem is that, sometimes, the interpretation is wrong. Your thoughts can give you a "false Identity". False Identity because it does not align with who you were created to be. It, instead, aligns with who your experiences told you you were.

So, the person who is hurt in a relationship has the thought that they aren't worth loving, and they believe it.

The person who closes a business has the thought that they are a failure, and they believe it.

The person struggling with their finances has the thought that they will always be poor, and they believe it.

The person who is abused has the thought that they deserved it, and they believe it.

The person whose parents get divorced has the thought that they are not worth loving, and they believe it.

The experiences may be painful, and I am sorry for the pain of your past, but the issue comes when we believe that our experiences aren't something we have gone through but who we are.

The third way that your thoughts create your life is by positioning you to walk in alignment with the person you were created to be.

Your thoughts are pre-rehearsed understandings of who you believe you are supposed to be.

The power in that is that, by changing your thoughts to be in alignment with who God says you are, you will find yourself transforming into that person.

IF YOU CAN MASTER YOUR THOUGHTS YOU CAN MASTER YOUR LIFE!

So, what do you focus on?

What do you think about it?

What tapes are playing in your head?

LIFE MASTERY SCRIPTURE: (Philippians 4:8) "Finally brethren, whatever things are true, whatever things are noble, whatever things are just, whatever things are pure, whatever things are lovely, whatever things are of good report, if there is any virtue and if there is anything praiseworthy – mediate on these things."

WHO YOU THINK YOU ARE YOU WILL BECOME

LIFE MASTERY

The more you "feed" your thoughts by creating a habit of rehearsing truth, the more you will see that truth and the person you are created to be show up in the experiences of your life.

It happens by meditating on, focusing on, and repetitiously practicing thoughts that reinforce your Identity.

It is the mental rehearsals that you practice. It is how you respond to challenges. It is the repetitive beliefs that you live from.

You have the power to develop positive responses, and with all of the knowledge, the next step is to put it into practice.

IF YOUR THOUGHTS ARE NOT REINFORCING YOUR IDENTITY THEN THEY ARE LYING TO YOU ABOUT YOUR IDENTITY

The secret is out. The truth is known. The strategy is in place. If you apply it, you can transform your life.

You have the truth, and that truth will make you free.

LIFE MASTERY

Chapter 9 – YOUR WORDS MATTER

I have a rhetorical question for you. What is the most powerful weapon that you don't know about?

I know, wacky, right?

How can you know about something you don't know about?

Let me show you.

Have you ever had someone put you down, belittle you, or tell you you couldn't do something that you were attempting to do?

I remember in my last year of Junior High, I had a teacher named Mr. Mordaunt. I was going to be going to a different high school than my classmates so that I could be a part of an ROTC program that the high school in my area did not offer.

I told Mr. Mordaunt what I was going to do, and he told me, "You aren't going to be able to accomplish that." For some reason, he felt it was his responsibility to let me know that I was going to fail.

I was bothered, a little irritated, and stunned that a teacher would tell me that. And I determined that I was going to prove him wrong. But, even though I did "accomplish it", I remember that man's words to this day.

On the other hand, have you ever had someone praise you, encourage you, or tell you could do something that you were attempting?

Sometimes, it is a small thing like telling you that they have faith in you. Sometimes, it is bigger, like telling you the character that they see inside of you.

To be honest, it is easier sometimes for me to remember the slights rather than the compliments.

One compliment that really blessed me and that stood out was when my wife told me that, according to her, I am one of the smartest people she knows. When she said it, I was both surprised and humbled.

I don't highlight this to pump myself up or put myself down but to demonstrate to you the most powerful weapon that you may not know about is the power of words.

This includes your words. Come to find out, we can be the source of our own issues or our own solutions.

Let's unpack this concept and see.

We have revealed the transformational strategy of Mastering your Thoughts, and I am hoping you are putting it into practice.

With that, the second transformational strategy, the one mentioned in the previous chapter, is Mastering your Words.

In your Life Mastery journey, as you focus on your thoughts, there is something that will naturally come after that.

That is, of course, the words that you speak.

Pretty straightforward, right?

But, even though that makes sense, you may ask, "What is the big deal with the words that I speak?"

LIFE MASTERY

LIFE MASTERY SCRIPTURE: (Pro. 18:21)
"Death and life are in the power of the
tongue, and those who love it will eat its
fruit."

(Lk. 6:45) "Out of the abundance of the heart
the mouth speaks."

There is power in the tongue, and if you use
that power to create empowering results, you
will have the life that you were created for.

What exactly does Mastering your Words do
in the context of mastering your life?

Before we get into what it does, you need to
realize that your words are "affirmations."
Just as your thoughts are "meditations."

And those affirmations, when they are
aligned with who you are created to be, will
do a few things.

The first is that they will build your character.
But you already know that.

As we talked about earlier, whether a person compliments or puts you down, let's be real; whether you compliment or put yourself down, it has an impact on your life.

The truth bomb I am giving you is this: either of them, compliment or put down, can and typically do have the outcome of shaping your Identity.

You see, words are used to build your authentic character or a false one.

And, not to put too fine of a point on it, as we discussed earlier, you have more of an impact on that through your words than others do simply by the words that come out of your mouth.

We are directing ourselves in who we believe we are all the time.

Every time we express something about ourselves out loud, we are "telling ourselves" who we believe we are.

Your words literally build your character.

So why not use words that align with your Identity? This gives you the power to give instructions to your brain on how to show up in your own life.

This leads me to the second design God has for your words/affirmations. It is to instruct you on how to live your life as the person you were created to be.

God has designed your brain in an interesting way to receive instructions from your words.

What this means is that whether you tell yourself disempowering words like, "I am so dumb," "I can't accomplish this", "I am not going to get this job," or empowering words like "I am going to win, this", "I have just the solution for this challenge" your brain hears those words and makes decisions, takes actions and hardwires mindsets to align with those words and make those things come to pass.

The design is inescapable. Your words will not only align with who you believe you are, but they will also instruct your brain to work towards the person you have described yourself to be with those same words.

I tell people all the time that if you speak with someone long enough, who they believe they are will always come out.

It will come out with how they answer, what words they use to describe themselves, and how they address the stress of their life.

You can pretend for a period of time, but, as my father would say, "when the rubber meets the road," who you believe you are will always come out.

That is why you may notice people who make the same bad decisions over and over again, whether it is in their relationships, financial choices, activities, or lifestyle.

The words we are using are either aligning with who we are created to be or aligning with the lies we have believed.

But your words can be a superpower; now that you are aware, you can use your words as the incredibly powerful tool God designed them to be.

Come on, somebody! That is exciting news.

Leading us smoothly to the third thing our affirmations do. As I have already said, your words always align with who you believe you are. But, as you continue to use words that align with who you are created to be, it creates a transformational momentum that changes your decisions, actions, and life.

Identity anyone?

You will either live from who you are created to be or who you think you are supposed to be.

The more we use words that align with the person we are created to be, the more we see that person show up in our lives.

Conversely, the more we use words that align with our pains, past experiences, and the lies we believe, the more that person shows up.

So, with all of that in mind, the question I have for you is, what slips out of your mouth when you are under stress when you have made a mistake, or when you are dealing with a challenge?

What are your automated declarations? You know, those things that just "slip out" without you even thinking. I call them the "always and nevers" of our lives.

"Why does something always go wrong?" "I am never going to be happy."

I have a secret for you. The way you describe your circumstance is the way you describe yourself. In describing your experiences, you are really describing the life you expect to have and the person you expect to be.

Are you a person who is meant for happiness and success?

Are you created for deep, meaningful relationships?

Are you a creative and clever businessperson who is on the rise?

And do your words reflect that, or do they reflect the challenge you are in the middle of?

YOUR WORDS SHAPE YOUR LIFE

The question to answer is, what directions are you giving your brain to follow?

What are your responses to stressful situations?

The real question is, what instructions are your **words** giving your brain to follow?

LIFE MASTERY SCRIPTURE: (James 3:4 – 5) "Look also at ships: although they are so large and are driven by fierce winds, they are turned by a very small rudder wherever the pilot desires. 5 Even so the tongue is a little member and boasts great things."

(Proverbs 21:23) "Whoever guards his mouth and tongue Keeps his soul from troubles."

Our words do two things. They reflect our thoughts and instruct our brains.

Whether your words are positive (empowering) or negative (disempowering), they are still affirming to your brain and your brain will align with them to ensure that they are true.

When your words align with who you are created to be, you will live the life you are created for.

Chapter 10 – ALL ABOUT ACTION

In my mid-twenties, I was renting a room from a friend, and it just so happened that one of her neighbors was a friend of hers who I met, flirted with, and fell in love with.

I have been married to that woman for over 30 years now.

Thinking about our relationship, I remember that, early on in our relationship, one of the ways we connected was through our shared passion for working out. This is still something we have continued to do all these years later. Not like in our 20s, of course, let's be real. But we are still active on purpose.

Of course, the truth is that the half-committed diet and exercise I employed to lose weight in my twenties doesn't work anymore. In fact, the older I get, the more every slice of cake, chocolate chip cookie, and bowl of chocolate fudge brownie ice cream has a negative effect on my waistline.

The one thing that has remained the same from the time that I first worked out to today is that you can think about getting in shape, and you can talk about getting in shape, but nothing happens until you actually modify your eating habits, get off your couch, and exercise.

There is a phrase that summarizes getting in shape, and this chapter, it is "Nothing happens until something happens."

We've been discussing transformational strategies in the last two chapters, and we've outlined Mastering your Thoughts and Mastering your Words.

Your thoughts are foundational for everything that you believe and everything you will do in your life.

On top of that, your words remind you of who you are and give your brain instructions to follow to see that person show up.

This leads us to our third transformational strategy, Mastering your Actions.

I am super excited about this conversation because now we are getting to the Activation part of the transformation.

The fact is that, no matter what your thoughts and words are, you will not have the life you are created for by just thinking and saying empowering things.

At the end of the day, transformation comes to life when you put action behind your thoughts and words.

That idea is worth unpacking because it is not just the fact that activation is an action that can lead to the results that you desire. It is the fact that the actions you take engage or hinder emotions that are in alignment with who you are created to be.

And those emotions reinforce your thoughts, which determine your words, which lead to your actions.

Let me prove it to you.

Imagine for a moment a person who is feeling dejected, defeated, or let down. As you picture them in your mind, tell me something. What does their body language look like?

Are their shoulders back or slouched?

Is their face smiling and alert or downcast and frowning?

Are their eyes confidently connecting with people or looking down?

We intuitively understand what a "dejected" or "confident" person looks like and can picture them in our minds. In other words, we know what specific emotions "look like," and we can even imitate them.

What we don't realize is that the converse is true also. If our emotions can be reflected by our body posture and facial expressions, then how we carry ourselves (body posture and facial expressions) can also change our emotions to align with our physical posture.

There are scientific studies on this subject and personal development programs that use this fact to manage emotions. Of course, there is a difference between managing emotions and

Mastering Actions, which we are, of course, going to detail in these upcoming pages.

But, back to Mastering your Actions. This particular transformational strategy is huge because it gives you the ability to "hack" your emotions to align with the person you are created to be and the life you are created for. Not just manipulate emotions that you don't like by changing posture.

In fact, that is just one aspect of actions.

Beyond posture and emotion regulation, you can build momentum, accelerate success & overcome negative input by the actions you take.

So, let's unpack the benefits of Mastering your Actions.

There are three primary benefits to Mastering your Actions.

The first is that Mastering your Actions enables you to frame your experiences, as we discussed above.

Your stature relays to your brain your confidence, concern, bravery, or timidity.

It is not a substitute or us pretending everything is okay, but when you align your countenance with the person you are created to be, you can change your emotions, biochemistry, and response.

Who you are created to be looks like something.

So, the question is, what does the person you are created to be look like lived out? The answer to that is your "I AM" statement, a descriptor of who you have been created to be. That person showing up in your life is what habituating your experiences looks like.

This leads me to the second benefit. Mastering your Actions habituates your responses.

It is not just showing up as the person you are created to be. There is this relationship between experience and response called automaticity that happens when you continue to Master your Actions repetitively.

Simply put, automaticity means that the more you proactively choose thoughts, words, and actions that align with who you are created to be, you actually create structures in your brain called neuro-plastic structures.

These structures, to be rather simplistic, facilitate automated responses to the circumstances of your life. And as a result, you will see the person you are created to be showing up more and more. Not just because of reminders that you give yourself but automatically as your "natural response" to the life that happens. Super exciting, right!

POSTURE REFLECTS PERSPECTIVE – It engages neuro-chemicals that engage the brain in positive ways and energizes us, assisting in decision-making, our sense of confidence, and our response to the "life that happens"

Which leads to the third benefit. Mastering your Actions reflects your Identity.

The truth is that your actions either reflect who were created to be or what your experiences, past & pains told you were.

The person of confidence and assurance can show up, or the person of inconsistency and insecurity can show up.

As a reminder, Identity is the framework for everything we do. The more we clearly know who we are, the more often that person will show up. And, as we mentioned previously, the more it will be an automatic response to the life we experience.

THERE IS POWER IN MOVEMENT!

LIFE MASTERY SCRIPTURE: (Lk. 6:45) "A good man out of the good treasure of his heart brings forth good; and an evil man out of the evil treasure of his heart brings forth evil..."

LIFE MASTERY

What actions are you taking?

More specifically, what actions are you taking when you are having to do something uncomfortable, when you are stressed, or when you lack a clear direction?

Is there a go-to "medication" that you are reaching for when life isn't going well? Ice cream? Long naps? Social media?

Apart from a Life Mastery journey, we all use some "medication" to make us feel better about the life we are living.

The other question I would ask you is, what body language do you have? Are you standing upright, leaning in, and walking with assurance? Or are your shoulders slouched, eyes down, and mouth frowning?

One of the quickest ways to change your bio-chemistry is to change your stance. As I stated earlier, there are whole personal development programs that are focused on the fact that you can change your emotional state and even bio-chemistry by changing your body language.

It matters.

It isn't the only thing that matters, like brakes aren't the only thing that matters in a car, but it is an integral part of your overall strategy to live a life of Life Mastery.

So, what do you look like during your day?

Now that I asked you, I bet you will be paying more attention to it.

What it really comes down to is that we are choosing one of two mindsets during our day. As the experiences of life are happening, we are either choosing to be a hero or a bystander.

The definition of being a hero is pretty straightforward. You show up as the person you were created to be, continually transforming your thoughts, words, and actions and living the life you are created for.

It doesn't mean that you are leaping tall buildings or catching bad people.

It is simply living your life by design, not by default.

It means that you are the person who takes ownership of your life, taking the actions that create the results you desire versus expecting someone else to do it or "fix it" for you.

What you are really doing by Mastering your Actions is building habits of success by living from your Identity, which is reinforcing your belief system.

We have gone over a lot of new revelations in these last few chapters, haven't we?

I can imagine that it is "frying your brain" so, to clear some of the smoke and summarize the three areas of our transformational strategy, you can think of it like this:

1) We have THOUGHTS in response to the life that happens and who we believe we are.
2) We use WORDS that align with who we believe we are, the thoughts we think, and which instruct us to live it out.

3) We have ACTIONS that align with our thoughts and words and enact the life we believe we are meant to live.

Remember that, in choosing an "empowering" action, you engage one of the quickest Life Mastery "hacks" to reset your emotions, which influences your Thoughts, Words, and Actions.

Here is how you know that you are Mastering your Actions. When your stature, posture & attitude are ones of confidence, strength & empowerment.

It is a matter of cause and effect. When you Master your Actions, you are proactively engaging your body to align with your belief system about yourself, your capability, and your outcome.

You also give a not-so-subtle reinforcement of who you believe you are. If you act like the "hero" in your own life, you will start to believe that you are the hero in your own life.

That is the power of Identity lived out.

It is not that we are pretending to be someone.

We start with who God created us to be and use the tools that engage us to align with that person.

It is not "fake it till you make it." It is UNCOVER it, so you can UNLEASH it.

This is because, neurologically, your posture positively or negatively affects your emotions, attitude, and outlook. As we have said, your biochemistry is affected by how you carry yourself and how you engage your emotions in response to your environment.

In a nutshell, we can wrap up Mastering Your Actions in two parts.

The first is answering the right question, and the second is taking the right actions.

The right question is, "What action would the **"Hero Me"** take?"

The right action is to understand that the person you were created to be looks like something and to show up as "that" person.

LIFE MASTERY

What does the person you are created to be look like in the "Hero" moments?

WE ARE EITHER A HERO OR A BYSTANDER IN OUR OWN LIFE

You were created to be the Hero. What does he/she look like? How does he/she respond? The answers to those questions make all of the difference in the world.

117

LIFE MASTERY

Chapter 11 - FREEDOM FROM OR FOR

I was in a group training a lifetime ago, and the speaker wanted to drive home a point on perspective. He showed us a picture that I am sure you have seen. As I looked at the picture, what I saw was a young woman dressed up in a hat and dress.

After a short while, he took a poll of the group to find out what they saw, and lo and behold, some of the people saw an old woman.

Crazy right? I thought so, also. Until he proceeded to outline the old woman in the picture, and I saw that woman, too.

The point of his exercise was to show that, depending on your perspective, you could be seeing different things

And that is exactly the same thing that can happen when we use the word "Freedom."

I have mentioned the word "Freedom" multiple times in our conversation and, to be honest, it is at the core of Life Mastery. You can never Master your Life if you are not walking in the Freedom that God has for you.

The problem is, like the picture of the two ladies, depending on your perspective, depending on where you come at it from, your understanding can be different, and, unfortunately, you can lose out on the deeper things that it has for you.

What I am saying is that the framework you have for understanding Freedom will determine the outcome you get from it.

There are two perspectives people will generally have when it comes to Freedom. They are either achieving Freedom from something, or they are achieving Freedom for something.

What do I mean?

Many times, we unknowingly limit our "Freedom" to overcoming the struggles & issues we have dealt with.

It is becoming free from the things you did wrong and the consequences of them.

You know, sin and death.

And there is a great blessing in that. After all, Jesus did die so that we would be free from the wages of our sin.

Do not misunderstand me. That is absolute Spiritual truth.

The question is, though, is that all?

Is the sum total of our Freedom only having forgiveness of our sins, as great as that is?

(John 8:36) "Therefore if the Son makes you free, you shall be free indeed."

When Jesus spoke of Freedom, in John 8:36, I believe there was more that God intended than just being saved from sins.

When you are living from a place of just being free from the sins and struggles of your past, you are living from who you used to be.

LIFE MASTERY

Basically, you are living to not repeat your mistakes.

That sounds more like life management to me.

What if God intended for us to not just be free from the sins of our past? What if He intended for us to be free for the life He created us to live?

Simply put, it is being free to be the person you were created to be, not just being free from the sins and mistakes of your past. We are not just overcoming sins. We are being unleashed into all that God has created us for.

How many of you know that focusing on mistakes isn't living? It is the difference between a regretful past and a promising future.

If you are living from a "Freedom For" perspective, you are free to be who you were created to be, and you live to engage the possibility & promise God has for you and your future.

Sounds so much more exciting to me and so much more like God.

At the risk of sounding too basic, it is the difference between living your life looking back or looking forward: a life on defense or a life on offense.

That difference is monumental.

Freedom from your past is living to make sure you don't make the same mistakes again, and that is a life of habits.

God has created you for way more than that.

It is not Freedom from but Freedom to become.

It is the difference between being a servant needing to earn your place or a son/daughter living from your place in the family.

It is habits versus inheritance.

It is work versus lifestyle.

LIFE MASTERY

You are created for a life of Freedom, not just a life with less mistakes.

If the Son sets you Free, you are Free indeed.

Change your mindset to match the intent of God, and you will be amazed at the results.

Chapter 12 - LIFE MASTERY IN EVERY AREA OF LIFE

WOW! You have done it, my friend. You have made it to the end of this book and, I believe, changed your life forever.

You can't unsee what you have seen or unlearn what you have learned.

You've bet on yourself and initiated some momentum that is going to lead you to accomplish some amazing things.

But before we end our conversation, I wanted to do a couple of things.

The first is to recognize that we have taken a journey through a bunch of different topics during our time together. We have talked about Life Mastery versus life management. We have unpacked Identity, Character, and Capacity. We have talked about the 3-Step Transformational Strategy: Mastering your Thoughts, Words, and Actions.

So, is that the end? Now that you have those items "in your arsenal" is that all you would ever need to be able to have the life you are created to have?

Well, not quite.

There is one subject that I want to share that, I believe, will tie it all together, but it starts with the question, "What's next?"

If Life Mastery actually looks like something lived out, the abundance of life that God promises, then it should look like that in every area of life.

(John 10:10) I have come that they may have life, and that they may have it more abundantly.

And, keep up with me: if it is supposed to look like something in every area of life, then what are those areas?

Smart question. Thanks for asking.

You know, like I do, that there is a big difference between having a strategy and having a "target" to point it towards.

And there is also a difference between knowing your Identity and actually living from that Identity in a meaningful way.

Really, what it comes down to is application. How do you apply the structure that God has given in this Life Mastery book?

To unpack that, I need to introduce you to the Five Areas of Life Mastery.

In the training, teaching, coaching, and living that I have done, I have come to see that there are five areas of life and Life Mastery.

What I have also discovered is that if we can live at the level that God has created us to in each of the five areas, we will have the abundant life that He created for us and created us for.

I am not saying that you will have success all of the time. But you can have fulfillment, which is the plan of God for your life.

God didn't create you to have success because, at its core, it is just being able to be diligent at a task, skill, or habit long enough to tip the scales of experience & efficiency so that you can accomplish something.

But, how many of you know that there are successful people all over the world who are successful at one or two things and a disaster at others?

Even more sad is the fact that you and I can probably name people we know or have been aware of who are successful and miserable.

Success is not the goal of God, even though we can and do achieve high levels of success as we follow His direction.

The goal isn't success, it is fulfillment!

Success is task mastery. Fulfillment is Life Mastery.

What does fulfillment look like? Fulfillment is you living from the person you were created to be and at the highest level that you were created for.

It is living, doing, and achieving the things that you were created for. It is effortless winning. Not that you don't put work into it. You are just not having to muster up energy and motivation but simply live from who you were created to be.

Fulfillment is the emotion you experience as you live your Life Mastery journey. Living from who you are created to be and having the life you are created for in every area of your life.

So, back to the topic at hand, the Five Areas of Life Mastery.

Without further ado, the Five Areas of Life Mastery are the Spiritual, Relational, Vocational, Physical, and Financial areas of life.

If you are living from who you are created to be (Identity) in each of these five areas, you will have the life you are created to have, and you will be fulfilled in every area of life.

LIFE MASTERY

Life Mastery lived out Spiritually. It is having the relationship with God that you are passionately pursuing or desperately need.

It is being connected to the eternal things of life. It is truly being a child of God in intellect and action rather than a son/daughter acting like a servant.

It is being in tune with God at all times and having an assurance of His direction and desire for you.

It is the fruit of the Spirit filling you to overflowing, not lacking, and praying desperately to receive it.

It is having the relationship with God that you dream of.

Life Mastery lived out Relationally. It is having meaningful relationships that are as honest, authentic, valued, and as safe as you have desired them to be.

It is being able to have hard conversations that improve the relationship instead of sabotaging it.

It is building towards something that you and your family/friends are both engaged and investing in.

It is them being a cheerleader in your life and you being one in theirs.

It is a place of voluntary vulnerability as you are teammates rather than competitors.

It is rich and blessed and challenging and worth it.

Life Mastery lived out Vocationally. It is not about a job, title, or business but about an impact.

It is about fulfilling the assignment that God has placed on your life.

It is investing the gifts, talents, and abilities that you have been created with so that the world is changed because you existed.
It is your unique contribution being lived out fully so that a legacy of your impact is in the world long after you are gone.

LIFE MASTERY

It is about dreaming big, living bigger, and leaving nothing on the table that God had in store through you to change the world.

Life Mastery lived out Physically. It is about being as healthy as you can, as long as you can, so that you are intellectually and physically vibrant for all of the days of your life.

It is about treating your body with the respect it needs and deserves so that it performs at its best at all times and in all circumstances.

It is about choosing good fuel, enjoying good food, challenging yourself and your physique to be at its best, and being prepared for the marathon of life.

It is about always engaging cognitively, not checking out because it is easy, and practicing the art of intellectual rigor.

Life Mastery lived out Financially. It is about having an abundance to invest in the things that are important to God and to you.

It is about living at the highest level you were created for, not the least that is safe.

It is about being a lender, not a borrower.

It is about maximizing the resources (talents) that God has entrusted you with so that people around you can see biblical philanthropy.

It is about buying back your time.

It is about creating security.

It is about setting up a legacy.

It is about the proper stewardship that God has entrusted to your care.

It is about the joy of receiving, the joy of giving, and the goal of being told, "Well done, good and faithful servant."

So, now that we have illustrated the framework for the Five Areas of Life Mastery, it is your turn.

I know what Life Mastery in each of these five areas looks like for me. I have goals, affirmations, and work that I put into each of them because I know my target.

But now is your time to create the target for your life.

What does Life Mastery look like for you, lived out in each of the five areas?

If your life was exactly how God created it to be in each of the five areas, what would that look like?

In being introduced to the five areas, I highly encourage you to take some time and to put your dream for those five areas "on paper." Whether it is on your computer, iPad, phone, journal, app, or diary, dictate it in writing and remind yourself of it daily.

This is a big deal.

There are so many people who, because they are in the middle of their dysfunction, never look above the fray.

That is a loss.

If you have come this far, I know that is not who you are.

So, how do we start? As always, you start with Identity.

By knowing who you are created to be, you will find it easier to see what your life looks like lived out Spiritually, Relationally, Vocationally, Physically, and Financially.

So, start by asking yourself the question, "What does my life look like lived out Spiritually, Relationally, Vocationally, Physically, and Financially.

As you start to get that answer, spend the time to write it down. Goals that are written down are achieved. Write it down in as much detail as you have.

Then **Revisit, Revise, Refine,** and **Record**.

Revisit –

My recommendation is to write down an "affirmation script" for each of the Five Areas of Life Mastery and then set it aside for a day.

Then, go back and read it again. It is a living document, and even after it is written down,

God is still transforming you. And, since He is, then maybe, just maybe, your Life Mastery goals will transform also.

Revise –

So, as you revisit the "scripts," revise them as it makes sense. Your first version is not set in stone but should be looked at as a first version. Because of that, you can revise it as often as you need so that it matches your intent and God's design in the current moment.

Refine –

For me, sometimes the first thing I write isn't necessarily the end product. So, with your scripts for the five areas, don't be afraid to strip away the things that sound nice and look holy but aren't honest or meant for you.

Record –

One of the most powerful tools I use in my ongoing Life Mastery journey is to record my affirmations so I can listen to them daily. I also have them written down so I can read them when it makes sense. But, by recording the affirmations, I have given myself the gift of mobility so that I can remind myself at those times when I can't read, like on my commute, when I am in a group, or in public areas.

It is a game changer.

If I can "talk straight" with you, I know that Life Mastery takes work. It isn't a magic formula or "abracadabra" statement that immediately transforms your life.

But it is a system that works.

So, why not invest your time, discover your goals, and go for it?

You will literally be transformed into the person God created you to be, and wouldn't that be magnificent?

What have you got to lose except to lose the things that have been holding you back?

Freedom is worth having, and Life Mastery is worth living. I promise you have it in you. So GO FOR IT!